the
Quiltmaker's Club

More Patterns
for Less

11 New Quilt Projects from Open Gate

Fat Quarter Winners

Monique Dillard

C&T PUBLISHING

Text and artwork copyright © 2011 by Monique Dillard

Artwork copyright © 2011 by C&T Publishing, Inc.

Publisher: Amy Marson

Creative Director: Gailen Runge

Acquisitions Editor: Susanne Woods

Editor: Lynn Koolish

Technical Editors: Carolyn Aune and Teresa Stroin

Copyeditor/Proofreader: Wordfirm Inc.

Cover/Book Designer: Kristy Zacharias

Production Coordinator: Jenny Leicester

Production Editor: Julia Cianci

Illustrator: Monique Dillard

Photography by Christina Carty-Francis and Diane Pedersen of C&T Publishing, Inc., unless otherwise noted

Published by C&T Publishing, Inc., P.O. Box 1456, Lafayette, CA 94549

Library of Congress Cataloging-in-Publication Data

Dillard, Monique, 1967-

Fat quarter winners : 11 new quilt projects from Open Gate / Monique Dillard.

    p. cm.

 ISBN 978-1-60705-190-9 (softcover)

1. Quilting--Patterns. 2. Patchwork--Patterns. 3. Quilts--Patterns. I. Title.

 TT835.D548 2011

 746.46--dc22

                    2010028182

Printed in China

10 9 8 7 6 5 4 3 2 1

Acknowledgments

I wouldn't be able to design my quilts without the support of my friends and family. I appreciate all the love and encouragement they give me. First, many thanks to my wonderful and talented friends who helped me piece the quilts in this book: Sue Glorch, Joyce Davis, and Kathy Rosecrance. Thank you to my fearless and creative machine quilters: LeAnne Olson, Sue Glorch, and Danette Gonzalez. Thanks to Katie Otto, who always has a way to turn my thoughts into the words I want to write. Thank you to my proofreaders, Kathy Rosecrance, Katie Otto, and Sue Glorch. Heartfelt thanks to my supportive and honest husband Bill—he doesn't let me get away with much! Thanks to my brother, Mike Ayotte; his wife, Tina Stewart; and my nieces, Holly and Blaire, who are always on my side, will listen to me when I need to talk, and keep me laughing. Deep gratitude to my mom and dad, John and Noreen Ayotte, who are always encouraging and excited with each new step I take. And thanks, Dad, for folding all those patterns!

Contents

Introduction

I designed this book specifically to use fat quarters for all the quilts. Fat quarters are the greatest invention that the quilting world has ever developed! Cut on the fold of a half yard of fabric, fat quarters are 18″ × 22″ (approximately, depending on the fabric manufacturer), and quilts using rotary-cut pieces can make incredible use of just about the whole fat quarter. I love how there is very little waste, and, depending on how a quilt is designed, two fat quarters of coordinating fabrics can make multiple blocks of a quilt as opposite images of each other. Any fabric left over from a fat quarter can be employed as part of the binding (see *Whist* on page 29). Whenever I have fat quarters left over on a project, I also like to use them as part of the backing.

All the quilts in this book are named after the card games I grew up playing with my grandma and parents. My husband and I got to know each other over the game of rummy, and we now have regular games of pinochle with my parents and friends. Playing cards and quilting are two of my favorite pastimes—what a great way to combine them with this book!

One of the extra features in this book is instructions that allow you to increase the size of your quilt by adding additional fat quarters. Want to make a twin-, queen-, or king-size quilt instead of a lap size? You can easily achieve this by creating extra blocks using additional fat quarters.

For example, my *Speed* quilt (page 26) instructs you to use 2 fat quarters to create 4 blocks. When you increase the size of the quilt, you increase it by multiples of 4 blocks (2 fat quarters for each 4 blocks). Therefore, if you want to make a twin-sized quilt, for example, you need 60 blocks (a total of 15 sets of 4 blocks, or a total of 30 fat quarters).

The quilts *King's Corner* (page 7) and *Whist* (page 29) are created with Square-in-a-Square units. Included in the directions are both the traditional instructions and the Fit to be Square method. I designed the Fit to be Square ruler to trim Square-in-a-Square blocks without bias edges. Using this ruler results in extremely accurate blocks.

The *Whist* (page 29), *Hearts* (page 32), and *Bridge* (page 36) quilts all have Flying Geese units. Included in the directions are both the traditional instructions and the Fit to be Geese method. I also designed the Fit to be Geese ruler, and my goal was to accurately trim Flying Geese with very little waste. See Resources (page 47) for more on Fit to be Square and Fit to be Geese rulers.

I very much enjoyed making all the quilts in this book; I hope you enjoy them as well. Hopefully you will be inspired to make one or two, or more, from this book. Quilting is addictive—quilting using fat quarters is even more so!

General Instructions

This chapter contains the instructions for making the commonly used blocks in this book: Half-Square Triangle units, as well as Flying Geese units and Square-in-a-Square units, which can be made using either of the two methods described below.

Half-Square Triangle Units

Draw a diagonal line from corner to corner on the back of a light square. Match the light square with a dark square, right sides together. Sew ¼" from both sides of the line. Cut the pieces apart on the line, and press toward the darker triangle. Please note that in the directions, Half-Square Triangle units are made larger than needed so you can square them to the exact size.

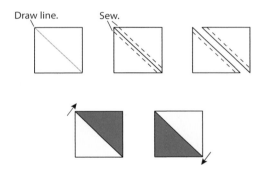

Flying Geese Units

Traditional Flying Geese Method

1. On the backs of 2 squares, draw a diagonal line from corner to corner.

Draw line.

2. Place a square on one end of a rectangle, right sides together. Sew directly on the line, and press in the direction of the arrow. You now have 3 layers of fabric in the corner. Trim the bottom 2 layers to ¼". Place the other square with a drawn line right sides together on the

rectangle. The square will overlap the first square by ¼". Sew directly on the line, and press in the direction of the arrow. Trim the bottom 2 layers to ¼".

Fit to be Geese Method

1. Cut a square diagonally once to create 2 triangles.

2. Cut a square diagonally twice to create 4 triangles.

3. Sew the long side of a triangle from Step 1 to a short side of a triangle from Step 2. Press in the direction of the arrow. Sew a matching triangle from Step 1 to the other side of the triangle from Step 2. Press in the direction of the arrow.

4. Line up the rooftop of the ruler along the seam, as shown, and trim the top of the Flying Geese unit using the Fit to be Geese ruler. Rotate the fabric 180°, and line up the trimmed edge with the size of Flying Geese unit that you are making. Trim the untrimmed edge. Rotate the piece 90°. Align the trimmed top and bottom edges of the unit between the red lines for the correct size on the ruler. Make sure that the center red dotted line is lined up where the seams cross, and trim. Use the dotted red line that is ¼" above the correct-sized black line. Finally, rotate the piece, and trim the other side by again sandwiching the piece between the lines for the correct size and the red dotted line in the center.

Trim.

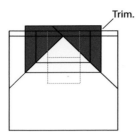

Trim.

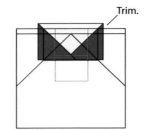

Trim.

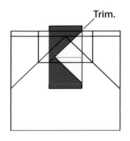

Trim.

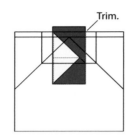

Square-in-a-Square Units

Traditional Square-in-a-Square Method

1. Cut 2 squares diagonally once to create 4 triangles.

2. Sew 2 triangles from Step 1 to the opposite sides of a square. Press toward the triangles. Sew 2 more of the triangles from Step 1 to the top and bottom of the square. Press toward the triangles.

Fit to be Square Method

1. Cut 2 squares diagonally once to create 4 triangles.

2. Sew 2 triangles from Step 1 to the opposite sides of a square. Press toward the triangles. Sew 2 more of the triangles from Step 1 to the top and bottom of the square. Press toward the triangles.

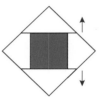 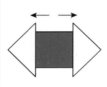

3. Line up the rooftop of the ruler along the seam, making sure that the vertical line runs through the bottom seams where they cross, and trim the top of the Fit to be Square unit. Rotate the piece 180°, and again line up the rooftop up along the seam while lining up the cut edge along the markings for the correct block size. Trim. Rotate the piece 90°. Line up the rooftop along the seam and the vertical line on the bottom where the seams cross. Note that the sides should fall along the markings for the correct size for your block. Trim. Rotate 180°, and line up the rooftop, the bottom measurement, and the sides. Trim.

Trim.

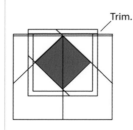

Trim.

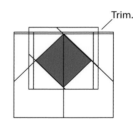

Trim.

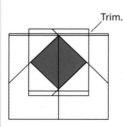

Trim.

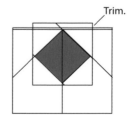

King's Corner

Designed and made by Monique Dillard.
Quilted by LeAnne Olson.

FINISHED BLOCK: 12″ × 12″
FINISHED QUILT (as shown): 66″ × 78″, 20 blocks

Information for alternate quilt sizes is on page 10.

Materials

- Light fabric: 10 fat quarters

- Dark fabric: 10 fat quarters

- 1st border: ⅝ yard

- 2nd border: ⅜ yard

- 3rd border: 1⅝ yards

- Binding: ⅝ yard

- Backing: 5 yards

- Batting: 74″ × 86″

- Optional: Fit to be Square ruler (page 5)

Cutting Instructions

Before beginning, match the light and dark fat quarters into pairs for piecing. Cut the light and dark fat quarters separately. Each light/dark pair makes 2 blocks.

LIGHT FAT QUARTERS
Fit to be Square method

- From each light fat quarter:

  Cut 1 strip 4½″ × width of fabric; cut into 4 squares 4½″ × 4½″, and cut each diagonally once to make 8 triangles (B).

  Cut 2 strips 3½″ × width of fabric; cut into 8 squares 3½″ × 3½″ (G) and 6 pieces 2″ × 3″ (E).

  Cut 1 strip 3″ × width of fabric; cut into 10 pieces 2″ × 3″ (E).

  Cut 1 strip 2½″ × width of fabric; cut into 8 squares 2½″ × 2½″ (C).

OR

Traditional Square-in-a-Square method

- From each light fat quarter:

  Cut 1 strip 3⅞″ × width of fabric; cut into 4 squares 3⅞″ × 3⅞″, and cut each diagonally once to make 8 triangles (B).

  Cut 2 strips 3½″ × width of fabric; cut into 8 squares 3½″ × 3½″ (G) and 6 pieces 2″ × 3″ (E).

Cut 1 strip 3″ × width of fabric; cut into 10 pieces 2″ × 3″ (E).

Cut 1 strip 2½″ × width of fabric; cut into 8 squares 2½″ × 2½″ (C).

DARK FAT QUARTERS

- From each dark fat quarter:

  Cut 1 strip 4¾″ × width of fabric; cut into 2 squares 4¾″ × 4¾″ (A) and 2 pieces 4½″ × 3½″ (F).

  Cut 1 strip 4½″ × width of fabric; cut into 6 pieces 4½″ × 3½″ (F).

  Cut 1 strip 2½″ × width of fabric; cut into 8 squares 2½″ × 2½″ (D).

FIRST BORDER

- Cut 7 strips 2½″ × width of fabric.

SECOND BORDER

- Cut 7 strips 1½″ × width of fabric.

THIRD BORDER

- Cut 8 strips 6½″ × width of fabric.

BINDING

- Cut 8 strips 2½″ × width of fabric.

Piecing

1. Make 6½″ × 6½″ Square-in-a-Square blocks.

For the Fit to be Square method (page 6), use 4 light triangles (B) cut from 2 squares 4½″ × 4½″ and a dark square 4¾″ × 4¾″ (A) for each unit. Repeat to make 2 from each light/dark fat quarter pair.

OR

For the traditional Square-in-a-Square method (page 6), use 4 light triangles (B) cut from 2 squares 3⅞″ × 3⅞″ and a dark square 4¾″ × 4¾″ (A) for each unit. Repeat to make 2 from each light/dark fat quarter pair.

Make 2 from each light/dark fat quarter pair.

2. Make 16 Half-Square Triangle units (page 5) from each of the light/dark fat quarter pairs using 8 light 2½″ × 2½″ squares (C) and 8 dark 2½″ × 2½″ squares (D). Trim the squares to 2″ × 2″.

Make 16 from each light/dark fat quarter pair.

3. Sew a light 2″ × 3″ piece (E) to the end of a Half-Square Triangle unit from Step 2 as shown. Be careful of the placement of the Half-Square Triangle units. Your piece should look exactly as shown. Press in the direction of the arrow. Repeat to make 16 from each light/dark fat quarter pair.

Make 16 from each light/dark fat quarter pair.

4. Sew 2 units from Step 3 together as shown. Press in the direction of the arrow. Repeat to make 8.

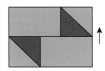

Sew together to make 8 from each light/dark fat quarter pair.

5. On the backs of the 8 dark 3½″ × 4½″ pieces (F) from each dark fat quarter, use the 45° mark on your ruler to draw diagonal lines as shown. Note that one line starts at the upper left corner, and the second line starts at the lower right corner. The lines must be at a 45° angle. Place a piece (F) right sides together on a unit from Step 4. Sew directly on the line. Cut ¼″ in from each sewn line. (Before cutting, check to make sure the sewn lines are in the correct direction.) Press each pair of units in opposite directions according to the arrows. Square each unit to 3½″ × 3½″. Repeat to make a total of 16 from each light/dark fat quarter pair.

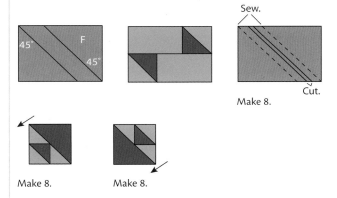

Make 16 from each pair.

6. Sew 2 units from Step 5 together as shown. Press in the direction of the arrow. Repeat to make a total of 8 from each light/dark fat quarter pair.

Make 8 from each pair.

7. Sew the blocks together using 4 light 3½″ × 3½″ squares (G), 1 unit from Step 1, and 4 units from Step 6. Press in the direction of the arrows. Square the blocks to 12½″ × 12½″. Repeat to make a total of 2 blocks per light/dark fat quarter pair to make the number of blocks for your desired quilt size. (For the quilt as shown on page 7, make 20 blocks.)

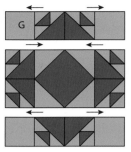 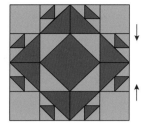

Make 2 per light/dark fat quarter pair.

ALTERNATE QUILT SIZES	TWIN	FULL/ QUEEN	KING
Number of blocks	24	42	64
Number of blocks wide by long	4 × 6	6 × 7	8 × 8
Finished size	66″ × 90″	90″ × 102″	114″ × 114″
YARDAGE			
Light fat quarters	12	21	32
Dark fat quarters	12	21	32
First border	⅝ yard	¾ yard	⅞ yard
Second border	⅜ yard	½ yard	½ yard
Third border	1⅞ yards	2 yards	2⅜ yards
Binding	¾ yard	⅞ yard	1 yard
Backing	5½ yards	8⅓ yards	10⅓ yards
Batting	74″ × 98″	98″ × 110″	122″ × 122″

Quilt Construction

Refer to the quilt photo on page 7 and to the Quilt Assembly Diagram. Follow the arrows for pressing direction.

1. Arrange the blocks, and sew the quilt together in rows. Press in the direction of the arrows.

2. Sew on the first border, the second border, and then the third border (see Borders, Quiltmaking Basics, page 45). Press toward the borders.

3. Quilt, bind, and enjoy! (See Quiltmaking Basics, pages 45–47.)

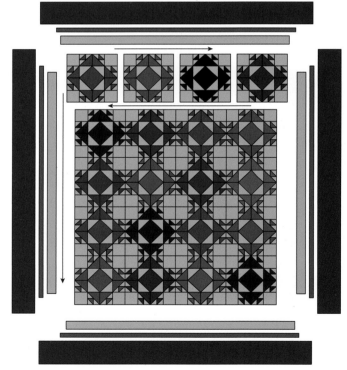

Quilt Assembly Diagram

Rummy

Designed by Monique Dillard.
Made by Monique Dillard and Sue Glorch.
Quilted by Danette Gonzalez.

FINISHED BLOCK: 8″ × 8″
FINISHED QUILT (as shown): 62″ × 78″, 48 blocks

Information for alternate quilt sizes is on page 14.

Materials

- Light fabric: 16 fat quarters

- Dark fabric: 16 fat quarters

- Inner border: ⅜ yard

- Outer border: 1⅝ yards

- Binding: ⅝ yard

- Backing: 5 yards

- Batting: 70″ × 86″

Cutting Instructions

Before beginning, match the light and dark fat quarters into pairs for piecing. Cut the light and dark fat quarters separately. Each light/dark pair makes 3 blocks.

LIGHT FAT QUARTERS

- From each light fat quarter:

  Cut 1 strip 3″ × width of fabric; cut into 3 squares 3″ × 3″ (G).

  Cut 3 strips 2½″ × width of fabric; cut into 24 squares 2½″ × 2½″ (E).

  Cut 2 strips 1½″ × width of fabric; cut into 6 pieces 1½″ × 3½″ (B) and 6 pieces 1½″ × 2½″ (C).

DARK FAT QUARTERS

- From each dark fat quarter:

  Cut 1 strip 3″ × width of fabric; cut into 3 squares 3″ × 3″ (H) and 6 squares 1½″ × 1½″ (A).

  Cut 5 strips 2½″ × width of fabric; cut into 12 pieces 2½″ × 4½″ (F) and 15 squares 2½″ × 2½″ (D).

INNER BORDER

- Cut 7 strips 1½″ × width of fabric.

OUTER BORDER

- Cut 8 strips 6½″ × width of fabric.

BINDING

- Cut 8 strips 2½″ × width of fabric.

Piecing

1. Sew a dark 1½″ × 1½″ square (A) to a light 1½″ × 3½″ piece (B). Press toward the dark square. Repeat to make a total of 6 from each light/dark fat quarter pair.

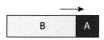

Make 6 from each light/dark fat quarter pair.

2. Sew a light 1½″ × 2½″ piece (C) to each side of a dark 2½″ × 2½″ square (D). Press toward the dark square. Repeat to make a total of 3 from each light/dark fat quarter pair.

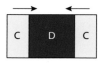

Make 3 from each light/dark fat quarter pair.

3. Sew the pieces from Step 1 and Step 2 together to make a square as shown. Press in the direction of the arrows. Square the block to 4½″ × 4½″. Repeat to make a total of 3 from each light/dark fat quarter pair.

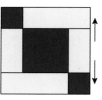

Make 3 from each light/dark fat quarter pair.

4. On the backs of 6 dark 2½″ × 2½″ squares (D), draw a diagonal line from corner to corner. Place a square, right sides together, on a light corner of the unit from Step 3. Sew directly on the drawn line, and press in the direction of the arrow. Trim the bottom 2 layers to ¼″. Sew another dark square on the opposite corner. Sew on the line, and press in the direction of the arrow. Trim the bottom 2 layers to ¼". Repeat this procedure for all 3 blocks made from each light/dark fat quarter pair.

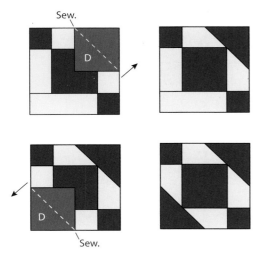

Make 3 from each light/dark fat quarter pair.

5. On the backs of the 24 light 2½" × 2½" squares (E), draw a diagonal line from corner to corner. Place a square on a dark 2½" × 4½" piece (F). Sew directly on the line, and press in the direction of the arrow. Trim the bottom 2 layers to ¼". Place another light square on the opposite corner, and sew directly on the line. Press in the direction of the arrow, and trim the bottom 2 layers to ¼". Watch the placement of the squares to make sure the piece looks exactly as shown. Repeat to make a total of 6 from each light/dark fat quarter pair.

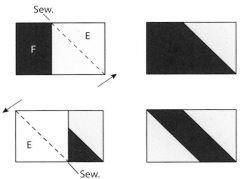

Make 6 from each light/dark fat quarter pair.

6. Place a light 2½" × 2½" square (E) with a drawn line on another dark 2½" × 4½" piece (F). Make sure that the diagonal line is heading in the opposite direction as in the pieces from Step 5. Sew directly on the line, and press in

the direction of the arrow. Trim the bottom 2 layers to ¼". Place another square with a drawn line on the opposite corner, and sew directly on the line. Press in the direction of the arrow, and trim the bottom layers to ¼". Repeat to make a total of 6 from each light/dark fat quarter pair.

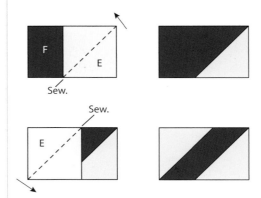

Make 6 from each light/dark fat quarter pair.

7. Make a Half-Square Triangle unit (page 5) using a light 3" × 3" square (G) and a dark 3" × 3" square (H). Trim the squares to 2½" × 2½". Repeat to make a total of 6 from each light/dark fat quarter pair.

Make 6 from each light/dark fat quarter pair.

8. Sew the blocks together using the units from Steps 4, 5, 6, and 7, and 2 dark 2½" × 2½" squares (D). Press in the direction of the arrows, and square the block to 8½" × 8½". Repeat to make 3 blocks from each light/dark fat quarter pair for the total number of blocks needed for your desired quilt size. (For the quilt as shown on page 11, make 48 blocks.)

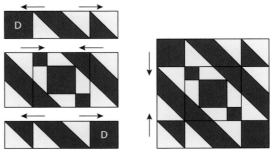

Make 3 blocks from each light/dark fat quarter pair.

Quilt Construction

Refer to the quilt photo on page 11 and to the Quilt Assembly Diagram. Follow the arrows for pressing direction.

1. Arrange the blocks, and sew the quilt together in rows. Press in the direction of the arrows.

2. Sew on the inner border and then the outer border (see Borders, Quiltmaking Basics, page 45). Press toward the borders.

3. Quilt, bind, and enjoy! (See Quiltmaking Basics, pages 45–47.)

Quilt Assembly Diagram

ALTERNATE QUILT SIZES	TWIN	FULL/ QUEEN	KING
Number of blocks	60	120	144
Number of blocks wide by long	6 × 10	10 × 12	12 × 12
Finished size	62″ × 94″	94″ × 110″	110″ × 110″
YARDAGE			
Light fat quarters	20	40	48
Dark fat quarters	20	40	48
Inner border	⅜ yard	½ yard	⅝ yard
Outer border	1¾ yards	2¼ yards	2⅜ yards
Binding	¾ yard	⅞ yard	1 yard
Backing	5¾ yards	8⅔ yards	10 yards
Batting	70″ × 102″	102″ × 118″	118″ × 118″

Gin Rummy

Designed and made by Monique Dillard.
Quilted by LeAnne Olson.

FINISHED BLOCK: 8″ × 8″
FINISHED QUILT (as shown): 44″ × 44″, 16 blocks

Information for alternate quilt sizes is on page 18.

Materials

- Light fabric: 4 fat quarters
- Brown fabric: 4 fat quarters
- Pink fabric: 4 fat quarters
- Inner border: ¼ yard
- Outer border and binding: 1⅓ yards
- Backing: 3 yards
- Batting: 52″ × 52″

Cutting Instructions

Before beginning, match a light, a pink, and a brown fat quarter together to make 4 sets for piecing. Each set of fat quarters makes 4 blocks. Cut the fat quarters separately.

LIGHT FAT QUARTERS

- From each light fat quarter:

    Cut 1 strip 3″ × width of fabric; cut into 4 squares 3″ × 3″ (H).

    Cut 4 strips 2½″ × width of fabric; cut into 32 squares 2½″ × 2½″ (F).

    Cut 3 strips 1½″ × width of fabric; cut into 8 pieces 1½″ × 3½″ (B) and 8 pieces 1½″ × 2½″ (C).

BROWN FAT QUARTERS

- From each brown fat quarter:

    Cut 2 strips 4½″ × width of fabric; cut into 16 pieces 4½″ × 2½″ (G).

    Cut 1 strip 2½″ × width of fabric; cut into 8 squares 2½″ × 2½″ (E).

PINK FAT QUARTERS

- From each pink fat quarter:

    Cut 1 strip 3″ × width of fabric; cut into 4 squares 3″ × 3″ (I).

    Cut 2 strips 2½″ × width of fabric; cut into 12 squares 2½″ × 2½″ (D).

    Cut 1 strip 1½″ × width of fabric; cut into 8 squares 1½″ × 1½″ (A).

INNER BORDER

- Cut 4 strips 1½″ × width of fabric.

OUTER BORDER AND BINDING

- Cut 5 strips 5½″ × width of fabric for outer border.

- Cut 5 strips 2½″ × width of fabric for binding.

Piecing

1. Sew a pink 1½″ × 1½″ square (A) to a light 1½″ × 3½″ piece (B). Press toward the pink square. Repeat to make a total of 8 from each pink and light combination.

Make 8 from each pink and light combination.

2. Sew a light 1½″ × 2½″ piece (C) to each side of a pink 2½″ × 2½″ square (D). Press toward the pink square. Repeat to make a total of 4 from each pink and light combination.

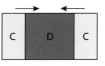

Make 4 from each pink and light combination.

3. Sew the pieces from Step 1 and Step 2 together to make a square as shown. Press in the direction of the arrows. Square the block to 4½″ × 4½″. Repeat to make a total of 4 from each pink and light combination.

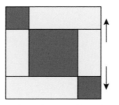

Make 4 from each pink and light combination.

4. On the backs of 8 brown 2½″ × 2½″ squares (E), draw a diagonal line from corner to corner. Place a square, right sides together, on the light corner of the unit you made in Step 3. Sew directly on the drawn line, and press in the direction of the arrow. Trim the bottom 2 layers to ¼″. Sew another brown square on the opposite corner. Sew on the line, and press in the direction of the arrow. Trim the bottom 2 layers to ¼″. Repeat this procedure with the 4 units made in Step 3.

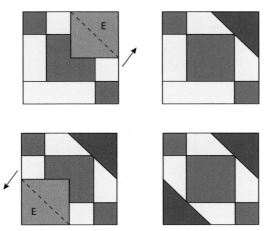

Repeat procedure with 4 units made in Step 3.

5. On the backs of the 32 light 2½″ × 2½″ squares (F), draw a diagonal line from corner to corner. Place a square with a drawn line on a brown 2½″ × 4½″ piece (G). Sew directly on the line, and press in the direction of the arrow. Trim the bottom 2 layers to ¼″. Place another drawn square on the opposite corner, and sew directly on the line. Press in the direction of the arrow, and trim the bottom 2 layers to ¼″. Watch the placement of the squares to make sure the piece looks exactly as shown. Repeat to make a total of 8 from each light and brown combination.

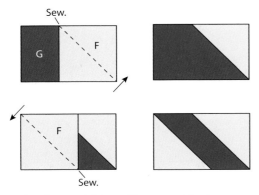

Make 8 from each light and brown combination.

6. Place a light 2½″ × 2½″ square (F) with a drawn line on another brown 2½″ × 4½″ piece (G). Make sure that the diagonal line is heading in the opposite direction as in the pieces from Step 5, as shown. Sew directly on the line, and press in the direction of the arrow. Trim the bottom 2 layers to ¼″. Place another square with a drawn line on the opposite corner, and sew directly on the line. Press in the direction of the arrow, and trim the bottom 2 layers to ¼″. Repeat to make a total of 8 from each light and brown combination.

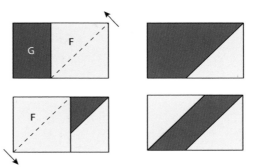

Make 8 from each light and brown combination.

7. Make 8 Half-Square Triangle units (page 5) using 4 light 3″ × 3″ squares (H) and 4 pink 3″ × 3″ squares (I). Trim the squares to 2½″ × 2½″. Repeat with each pink and light combination.

Make 8 from each pink and light combination.

8. Sew a block together using the units from Steps 4, 5, 6, and 7, and 2 pink squares 2½″ × 2½″ (D). Press in the direction of the arrows, and square the block to 8½″ × 8½″. Repeat to make 4 blocks per color combination for the total number of blocks needed for your desired quilt size. (For the quilt as shown on page 15, make 16 blocks.)

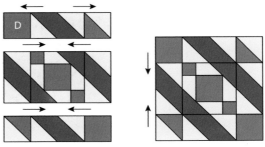

Make 4 blocks per color combination.

Quilt Construction

Refer to the quilt photo on page 15 and to the Quilt Assembly Diagram. Follow the arrows for pressing direction.

1. Arrange the blocks, and sew the quilt together in rows. Press in the direction of the arrows.

2. Sew on the inner border and then the outer border (see Borders, Quiltmaking Basics, page 45). Press toward the borders.

3. Quilt, bind, and enjoy! (See Quiltmaking Basics, pages 45–47.)

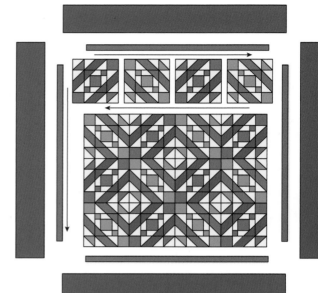

Quilt Assembly Diagram

ALTERNATE QUILT SIZES	LAP	TWIN	QUEEN/FULL	KING
Number of blocks	48	60	120	144
Number of blocks wide by long	6 × 8	6 × 10	10 × 12	12 × 12
Finished size	62″ × 78″	62″ × 94″	94″ × 110″	110″ × 110″
YARDAGE				
Light fat quarters	12	15	30	36
Brown fat quarters	12	15	30	36
Pink fat quarters	12	15	30	36
Inner border	⅓ yard	⅜ yard	½ yard	⅝ yard
Outer border & binding	2¼ yards*	2½ yards*	3 yards*	3½ yards*
Backing	5 yards	5¾ yards	8⅔ yards	10 yards
Batting	70″ × 86″	70″ × 102″	102″ × 118″	118″ × 118″

Note that for the larger sizes the outer border is cut 6½″.

Spades

Designed and made by Monique Dillard.
Quilted by LeAnne Olson.

FINISHED BLOCK: 7½″ × 7½″
FINISHED QUILT (as shown): 42½″ × 63½″, 38 blocks

Information for alternate quilt sizes is on page 22.

Materials

- Light fabric: 10 fat quarters
- Dark fabric: 10 fat quarters
- Binding: ½ yard
- Backing: 3 yards
- Batting: 50″ × 71″

Cutting Instructions

Before cutting, match the light and dark fat quarters into pairs, and cut the pairs with right sides together. Each light/dark pair makes 4 blocks.

LIGHT AND DARK FAT QUARTERS

- Cut 1 strip 6⅞″ × width of fabric; cut into 1 setting triangle 6⅞″ as shown.

- Cut 1 strip 6¾″ × width of fabric; cut into 2 squares 5⅞″ × 5⅞″ (E and F), and cut each diagonally once; then cut 4 squares 3⅜″ × 3⅜″ (C and D), and cut each diagonally once.

- Cut 1 strip 3½″ × width of fabric; cut into 6 squares 3½″ × 3½″ (A and B).

Note: If you are short a 3½″ × 3½″ square, use the leftover from the 6⅞″ strip to cut the extra square.

BINDING

- Cut 6 strips 2¼″ × width of fabric.

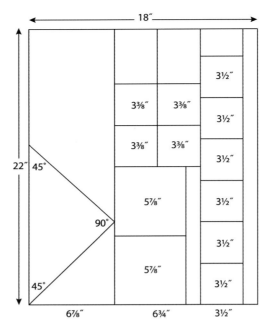

Fat Quarter Cutting Diagram

Piecing

1. Make 12 Half-Square Triangle units (page 5) using 6 light 3½″ × 3½″ squares (A) and 6 dark 3½″ × 3½″ squares (B). Trim the squares to 3″ × 3″. Repeat for a total of 12 from each light/dark fat quarter pair.

Make 12 Half-Square Triangle units from each light/dark fat quarter pair.

2. Sew a dark triangle cut from a 3⅜″ × 3⅜″ square (D) to a Half-Square Triangle unit from Step 1. Press in the direction of the arrow. Sew another dark triangle cut from a 3⅜″ × 3⅜″ square (D) to the other side. Press in the direction of the arrows. Repeat for a total of 4 from each light/dark fat quarter pair.

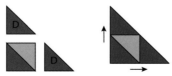

Make 4 from each light/dark fat quarter pair.

3. Sew a light triangle cut from a 5⅞″ × 5⅞″ square (E) to the piece from Step 2 as shown. Press 2 units in one direction and the other 2 in the opposite direction. Square the block to 5½″ × 5½″. Repeat to make 4 from each light/dark fat quarter pair.

Make 4 from each light/dark fat quarter pair.

4. Sew a light triangle cut from a 3⅜″ × 3⅜″ square (C) to a Half-Square Triangle unit from Step 1, watching the placement of the pieces. Press in the direction of the arrow. Repeat to make a total of 4 from each light/dark fat quarter pair.

Make 4 from each light/dark fat quarter pair.

5. Sew a light triangle cut from a 3⅜″ × 3⅜″ square (C) to a Half-Square Triangle unit from Step 1, watching the placement of the pieces. Press in the direction of the arrows. Repeat to make a total of 4 from each light/dark fat quarter pair.

Make 4 from each light/dark fat quarter pair.

6. Sew the units from Steps 4 and 5 to the unit from Step 3. Press in the direction of the arrows. Repeat to make a total of 4 from each light/dark fat quarter pair.

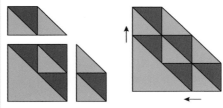

Combine units from Steps 3, 4, and 5. Make 4 total from each light/dark fat quarter pair.

7. Sew a triangle cut from a dark 5⅞″ × 5⅞″ square (F) to a unit from Step 6. Press 2 of the blocks in one direction and 2 in the opposite direction. Square the block to 8″ × 8″. Repeat the entire procedure to make 4 blocks per fat quarter pair for the total number of blocks needed for your desired quilt size. (For the quilt as shown on page 19, make 40 blocks.)

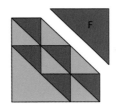

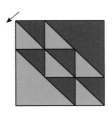 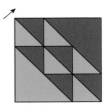

Make 4 from each light/dark fat quarter pair.

Quilt Construction

Refer to the quilt photo on page 19 and to the Quilt Assembly Diagram. Follow the arrows for pressing direction.

1. Arrange the blocks, and sew the quilt together in diagonal rows. Note that you will have extra blocks when constructing the quilt. Press in the direction of the arrows.

2. The 6⅞" side and corner setting triangles are larger than needed. Using the diagram as your guide, trim the quilt top, leaving a ¼" seam allowance outside the intersections of the diagonal seam.

Hint: To keep the sides from distorting while machine quilting, sew a basting stitch ⅛" around the edge of the quilt.

3. Quilt, bind, and enjoy! (See Quiltmaking Basics, pages 45–47.)

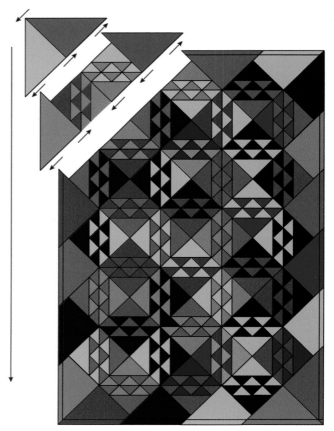

Quilt Assembly Diagram

ALTERNATE QUILT SIZES	TWIN	FULL/ QUEEN	KING
Number of blocks	82*	127*	180
Finished size	63½" × 85"	85" × 95½"	106" × 106"
YARDAGE			
Light fat quarters	21	32	45
Dark fat quarters	21	32	45
Binding	⅝ yard	¾ yard	⅞ yard
Backing	5¼ yards	8 yards	9¾ yards
Batting	71" × 93"	93" × 103"	114" × 114"

Note that you will have extra setting triangles. For the twin size you will have 2 extra blocks, and for the full/queen size you will have 1 extra block.

Pinochle

Designed and made by Monique Dillard.
Quilted by LeAnne Olson.

FINISHED BLOCK: 16″ × 16″
FINISHED QUILT (as shown): 60″ × 76″, 12 blocks

Information for alternate quilt sizes is on page 25.

Materials

- Light fabric: 12 fat quarters
- Dark fabric: 12 fat quarters
- Border: 1⅝ yards
- Binding: ⅝ yard
- Backing: 4 yards
- Batting: 68″ × 84″

Cutting Instructions

Before cutting, match the light and dark fat quarters into pairs, and cut the pairs with right sides together. Each light/dark pair makes 1 block.

LIGHT AND DARK FAT QUARTERS

- From each light/dark fat quarter pair:

  Cut 3 strips 3″ × width of fabric; cut into 16 squares 3″ × 3″ (A and B).

  Cut 1 strip 5″ × width of fabric; cut into 4 squares 5″ × 5″ (C and D).

BORDER

- Cut 8 strips 6½″ × width of fabric.

BINDING

- Cut 8 strips 2½″ × width of fabric.

Piecing

1. Make 32 Half-Square Triangle units (page 5) from each pair of light and dark fat quarters using 16 light 3″ × 3″ squares (A) and 16 dark 3″ × 3″ squares (B). Trim the squares to 2½″ × 2½″. Repeat using the remaining pairs of light and dark 3″ × 3″ squares.

Make 32 from each light/dark fat quarter pair.

2. Make 8 Half-Square Triangle units from each pair of light and dark fat quarters using 4 light 5″ × 5″ squares (C) and 4 dark 5″ × 5″ squares (D). Trim the squares to 4½″ × 4½″. Repeat using the remaining light and dark 5″ × 5″ squares.

Make 8 from each light/dark fat quarter pair.

3. Sew all the 2½″ Half-Square Triangle units from Step 1 into groups of 4, mixing up the lights and darks. Press in the direction of the arrows. Square the units to 4½″ × 4½″. Repeat to make 8 units for each block.

Sew Half-Square Triangle units into groups of 4.

4. Sew together the units from Step 2 and Step 3. Press in the direction of the arrows. Square the combined units to 8½″ × 8½″. Repeat to make 4 combined units for each block.

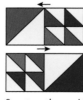

Sew together units from Steps 2 and 3.

5. Make the blocks using all the combined units from Step 4. Press in the direction of the arrows. Square the blocks to 16½″ × 16½″. Repeat the entire procedure to make the total number of blocks needed for your desired quilt size. (For the quilt as shown on page 23, make 12 blocks.)

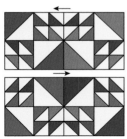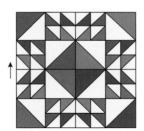

Make blocks.

Quilt Construction

Refer to the quilt photo on page 23 and to the Quilt Assembly Diagram. Follow the arrows for pressing direction.

1. Arrange the blocks, and sew the quilt together in rows. Press in the direction of the arrows.

2. Sew on the outer border (see Borders, Quiltmaking Basics, page 45). Press toward the border.

3. Quilt, bind, and enjoy! (See Quiltmaking Basics, pages 45–47.)

Quilt Assembly Diagram

ALTERNATE QUILT SIZES	TWIN	FULL/ QUEEN	KING
Number of blocks	15	30	36
Number of blocks wide by long	3 × 5	5 × 6	6 × 6
Finished size	60″ × 92″	92″ × 108″	108″ × 108″
YARDAGE			
Light fat quarters	15	30	36
Dark fat quarters	15	30	36
Border	1¾ yards	2⅛ yards	2¼ yards
Binding	⅝ yard	⅞ yard	1 yard
Backing	5⅔ yards	8½ yards	10 yards
Batting	68″ × 100″	100″ × 116″	116″ × 116″

Speed

Designed by Monique Dillard.
Made by Kathy Rosecrance.
Quilted by LeAnne Olson.

FINISHED BLOCK: 8″ × 8″
FINISHED QUILT (as shown): 60″ × 76″, 48 blocks

Information for alternate quilt sizes is on page 28.

Materials

- Light fabric: 12 fat quarters

- Dark fabric: 12 fat quarters

- Border: 1⅝ yards

- Binding: ⅝ yard

- Backing: 4 yards

- Batting: 68″ × 84″

Cutting Instructions

Before cutting, match the light and dark fat quarters into pairs, and cut the pairs with right sides together. Each light/dark pair makes 4 blocks.

LIGHT AND DARK FAT QUARTERS

- From each light/dark fat quarter pair:

  Cut 4 strips 3″ × width of fabric; cut into 24 squares 3″ × 3″ (A and B).

  Cut 1 strip 5½″ × width of fabric; cut into 2 squares 5½″ × 5½″ (C and D).

BORDER

- Cut 8 strips 6½″ × width of fabric.

BINDING

- Cut 8 strips 2½″ × width of fabric.

Piecing

1. Sew the blocks in light and dark pairs. Make 48 Half-Square Triangle units (page 5) from each pair of light and dark fat quarters using 24 light 3″ × 3″ squares (A) and 24 dark 3″ × 3″ squares (B). Trim the squares to 2½″ × 2½″.

Make 48 from each light/dark fat quarter pair.

2. Match 5½″ squares (C) of the same light fabric from Step 1 with 5½″ squares (D) of the same dark fabric from Step 1. On the backs of the light squares, draw a diagonal line from corner to corner. Sew ¼″ from both sides of the drawn line. Cut directly on the line. Press toward the dark. Rotate a resulting piece 180°, and place it right sides together on another piece. On the back, draw a diagonal line from corner to corner. Sew ¼″ from both sides of the drawn line. Cut directly on the line. Press in the direction of the arrows. Square to 4½″ × 4½″. Repeat to make a total of 4 Quarter-Square Triangle units of the same light and dark pair from each pair of light and dark fat quarters.

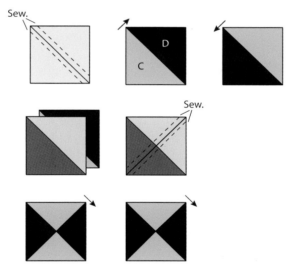

Make 4 from each light/dark fat quarter pair.

3. Sew the pieces from Step 1 and Step 2 together as shown. Press in the direction of the arrows. Square the blocks to 8½″ × 8½″. Repeat to make 4 blocks per light/dark fat quarter pair for the total number of blocks for your desired quilt size. (For the quilt as shown on page 26, make 48 blocks.)

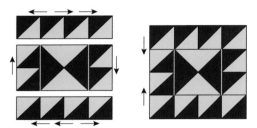

Make 4 blocks per light/dark fat quarter pair.

4. Repeat Steps 1–3 using the remaining pairs of light and dark fat quarters.

Quilt Construction

Refer to the quilt photo on page 26 and to the Quilt Assembly Diagram. Follow the arrows for pressing direction.

1. Arrange the blocks, and sew the quilt together in rows. Press in the direction of the arrows.

2. Sew on the outer border (see Borders, Quiltmaking Basics, page 45). Press toward the border.

3. Quilt, bind, and enjoy! (See Quiltmaking Basics, pages 45–47.)

Quilt Assembly Diagram

ALTERNATE QUILT SIZES	TWIN	FULL/ QUEEN	KING
Number of blocks	60	120	144
Number of blocks wide by long	6 × 10	10 × 12	12 × 12
Finished size	60″ × 92″	92″ × 108″	108″ × 108″
YARDAGE			
Light fat quarters	15	30	36
Dark fat quarters	15	30	36
Border	1¾ yards	2¼ yards	2⅜ yards
Binding	⅝ yard	⅞ yard	1 yard
Backing	5⅔ yards	8½ yards	10 yards
Batting	68″ × 100″	100″ × 116″	116″ × 116″

Whist

Designed and made by Monique Dillard.
Quilted by LeAnne Olson.

FINISHED BLOCK: 8½″ × 8½″
FINISHED QUILT (as shown): 51″ × 68″, 48 blocks

Information for alternate quilt sizes is on page 31.

Materials

- Light fabric: 12 fat quarters
- Dark fabric: 12 fat quarters
- Binding: ⅝ yard or use leftover fat quarters
- Backing: 3½ yards or use 15 fat quarters
- Batting: 59″ × 76″
- Optional: Fit to be Geese ruler and Fit to be Square ruler (page 5)

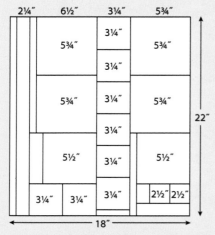

Fit to be Square and Fit to be Geese Fat Quarter Cutting Diagram

Cutting Instructions

Before cutting, match the light and dark fat quarters into pairs, and cut with right sides together. Each light/dark pair makes 4 blocks: 2 with light geese and 2 with dark geese.

LIGHT AND DARK FAT QUARTERS
Fit to be Geese method and Fit to be Square method

- From each light/dark fat quarter pair:

    Cut 1 strip 5¾″ × width of fabric; cut into 2 squares 5¾″ × 5¾″ (D), and cut each diagonally once; cut 1 square 5½″ × 5½″ (A), and cut diagonally twice; and cut 2 squares 2½″ × 2½″ (C).

    Cut 1 strip 3¼″ × width of fabric; cut into 6 squares 3¼″ × 3¼″ (B), and cut each diagonally once.

    Cut 1 strip 6½″ × width of fabric; cut into 2 squares 5¾″ × 5¾″ (D), and cut each diagonally once; cut 1 square 5½″ × 5½″ (A), and cut diagonally twice; and cut 2 squares 3¼″ × 3¼″ (B), and cut each diagonally once.

    Cut 1 strip 2¼″ × width of fabric for binding (optional).

OR

Traditional method

- From each light/dark fat quarter pair:

    Cut 1 strip 5⅛″ × width of fabric; cut into 4 squares 5⅛″ × 5⅛″ (D), and cut each diagonally once.

    Cut 1 strip 4½″ × width of fabric; cut into 8 pieces 2½″ × 4½″ (A).

    Cut 3 strips 2½″ × width of fabric; cut into 18 squares 2½″ × 2½″ (B and C).

    Cut 1 piece 2¼″ × 15″ for binding (optional).

BINDING

- *(Optional; cut if not using strips from the fat quarters)*
- Cut 7 strips 2¼″ × width of fabric.

Piecing

1. Make 8 Flying Geese units measuring 4½″ × 2½″ from each pair of light and dark fat quarters.

For the Fit to be Geese method (page 5), use 16 light triangles cut from 3¼″ × 3¼″ squares cut diagonally once (B) and 8 dark triangles cut from 2 squares 5½″ × 5½″ cut diagonally twice (A).

OR

For the traditional method (page 5), use 16 light 2½″ × 2½″ squares (B) and 8 dark 2½″ × 4½″ pieces (A).

Make 8 from each light/dark fat quarter pair.

2. Construct the center of each block using a light 2½″ × 2½″ square (C) and 4 Flying Geese units from Step 1. Sew the first Flying Geese unit only halfway on the light 2½″ × 2½″ square as shown. Press toward the Flying Geese unit. Rotate, sew, and press the remaining Flying Geese units as shown. Finally, sew the last half-seam. Square the piece to 6½″ × 6½″. Make a total of 2 with the same light center per pair of light and dark fat quarters.

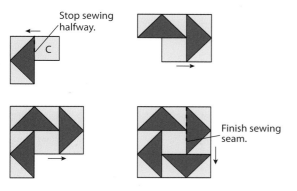

Make 2 from each light/dark fat quarter pair.

3. Make blocks measuring 9″ × 9″.

For the Fit to be Square method (page 6), use 4 dark triangles cut from 2 squares 5¾″ × 5¾″ (D) and a unit from Step 2. Make 2 blocks with the same light/dark fat quarters.

OR

For the traditional Square-in-a-Square method (page 6), use 4 dark triangles cut from 2 squares 5⅛″ × 5⅛″ (D) and a unit from Step 2. Make 2 blocks with the same light/dark fat quarters.

Make 2 per light/dark fat quarter pair.

4. Repeat Steps 1–3 reversing the lights and the darks to make 2 blocks per pair of light and dark fat quarters.

Block with reversed lights and darks

5. Repeat the entire procedure to make the total number of blocks for your desired quilt size. (For the quilt as shown on page 29, make 48 blocks.)

Quilt Construction

Refer to the quilt photo on page 29 and to the Quilt Assembly Diagram. Follow the arrows for pressing direction.

1. Arrange the blocks, and sew the quilt together in rows.

2. Press in the direction of the arrows.

3. Quilt, bind, and enjoy! (See Quiltmaking Basics, pages 45–47.)

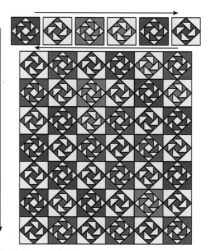

Quilt Assembly Diagram

ALTERNATE QUILT SIZES	TWIN	FULL/ QUEEN	KING
Number of blocks	70*	120	169*
Number of blocks wide by long	7 × 10	10 × 12	13 × 13
Finished size	59½″ × 85″	85″ × 102″	110½″ × 110½″
YARDAGE			
Light fat quarters	18	30	43
Dark fat quarters	18	30	43
Binding (optional)	⅔ yard	⅞ yard	1 yard
Backing	5¼ yards	8 yards	10 yards
Batting	68″ × 93″	93″ × 110″	119″ × 119″

There will be 2 leftover blocks for the twin size and 3 leftover blocks for the king size.

Hearts

Designed by Monique Dillard.
Made by Joyce Davis.
Quilted by LeAnne Olson.

FINISHED BLOCK: 9″ × 9″
FINISHED QUILT (as shown): 60″ × 78″, 35 blocks

Information for alternate quilt sizes is on page 35.

Materials

- Light fabric: 7 fat quarters

- Pink fabric: 7 fat quarters

- Red fabric: 7 fat quarters

- Brown fabric: 7 fat quarters

- Inner border: ½ yard

- Outer border: 1½ yards

- Binding: ⅝ yard

- Backing: 5 yards

- Batting: 68″ × 86″

- Optional: Fit to be Geese ruler (page 5)

Cutting Instructions

Before beginning, match the light, pink, red, and brown fat quarters into sets for piecing. Cut the fat quarters separately. Each set of fat quarters will make 5 blocks.

LIGHT FAT QUARTERS

Fit to be Geese method

- From each light fat quarter:

  Cut 3 strips 2¾″ × width of fabric; cut into 20 squares 2¾″ × 2¾″, and cut diagonally once (A).

  Cut 2 strips 4½″ × width of fabric; cut into 10 pieces 4½″ × 3½″ (F).

OR

Traditional method

- From each light fat quarter:

  Cut 4 strips 2″ × width of fabric; cut into 40 squares 2″ × 2″ (A).

  Cut 2 strips 4½″ × width of fabric; cut into 10 pieces 4½″ × 3½″ (F).

PINK FAT QUARTERS

- From each pink fat quarter:

  Cut 1 strip 3½″ × width of fabric; cut into 5 squares 3½″ × 3½″ (G).

RED FAT QUARTERS

Fit to be Geese method

- From each red fat quarter:

  Cut 3 strips 2¾″ × width of fabric; cut into 20 squares 2¾″ × 2¾″, and cut diagonally once (C).

  Cut 2 strips 3″ × width of fabric; cut into 20 pieces 2″ × 3″ (D).

OR

Traditional method

- From each red fat quarter:

  Cut 4 strips 2″ × width of fabric; cut into 40 squares 2″ × 2″ (C).

  Cut 2 strips 3″ × width of fabric; cut into 20 pieces 2″ × 3″ (D).

BROWN FAT QUARTERS

Fit to be Geese method

- From each brown fat quarter:

  Cut 3 strips 4½″ × width of fabric; cut into 10 squares 4½″ × 4½″, and cut diagonally twice (B); from the remaining strips cut 10 squares 2″ × 2″ (E).

  Cut 1 strip 2″ × width of fabric; cut into 10 squares 2″ × 2″ (E).

OR

Traditional method

- From each brown fat quarter:

  Cut 4 strips 3½″ × width of fabric; cut into 40 pieces 2″ × 3½″ (B).

  Cut 2 strips 2″ × width of fabric; cut into 20 squares 2″ × 2″ (E).

INNER BORDER

- Cut 6 strips 2″ × width of fabric.

OUTER BORDER

- Cut 8 strips 6½″ × width of fabric.

BINDING

- Cut 8 strips 2½″ × width of fabric.

Piecing

1. Make 20 Flying Geese units measuring 2″ × 3½″ for the pair of light and brown fat quarters in each fabric combination.

For the Fit to be Geese method (page 5), use 40 light triangles cut from squares 2¾″ × 2¾″ cut diagonally once (A) and 20 brown triangles cut from 5 squares 4½″ × 4½″ cut diagonally twice (B).

OR

For the traditional method (page 5), use 40 light squares 2″ × 2″ (A) and 20 brown pieces 2″ × 3½″ (B).

Make 20 from each pair of light and brown fat quarters.

2. Make 20 Flying Geese units measuring 2″ × 3½″ for the pair of red and brown fat quarters in each fabric combination.

For the Fit to be Geese method (page 5), use 40 red triangles cut from 2¾″ × 2¾″ squares cut diagonally once (C) and 20 brown triangles cut from 4½″ × 4½″ squares cut diagonally twice (B).

OR

For the traditional method (page 5), use 40 red squares 2″ × 2″ (C) and 20 brown 2″ × 3½″ pieces (B).

Make 20 from each pair of red and brown fat quarters.

3. Sew the Flying Geese units from Steps 1 and 2 together. Press in the direction of the arrow. Square the resulting units to 3½″ × 3½″.

Sew units together.

4. Sew a red 2″ × 3″ piece (D) to a brown 2″ × 2″ square (E). Press toward the brown. Repeat to make a total of 20 from the pair of red and brown fat quarters in each fabric combination. Rotate a set, and sew them together as shown. Watch the placement of the squares. On the back of the piece, snip ¼″ in the center seam so that you can press half the seam up and the other half down.

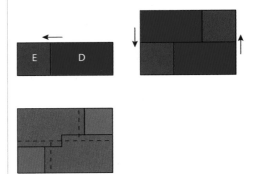

Make 10 from each pair of red and brown fat quarters.

5. On the backs of the light 4½″ × 3½″ pieces (F), use the 45° mark on your ruler to draw 2 diagonal lines as shown. Note that one line starts at the upper left corner, and the second line starts at the lower right corner, and the lines must be at a 45° angle. Place the rectangles with the drawn lines right sides together on the units from Step 4. Sew exactly on each line, and cut ¼″ in from the lines. (Before cutting, check to make sure the sewn lines are in the correct direction.) Press toward the light fabric. Square to 3½″ × 3½″. Repeat to make a total of 20 units from each fabric combination.

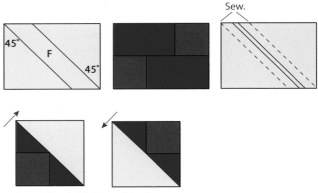

Make 20 of each fabric combination.

6. Sew together the block using the units from Steps 3 and 5 and a pink 3½" × 3½" square (G). Press in the direction of the arrows. Square the block to 9½" × 9½". Make 5 blocks of each fabric combination. Repeat the entire procedure to make the number of blocks needed for your desired quilt size. (For the quilt as shown on page 32, make 35 blocks.)

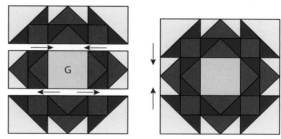

Make 5 of each fabric combination.

Quilt Construction

Refer to the quilt photo on page 32 and to the Quilt Assembly Diagram. Follow the arrows for pressing direction.

1. Arrange the blocks, and sew the quilt together in rows. Press in the direction of the arrows.

2. Sew on the inner border and then the outer border (see Borders, Quiltmaking Basics, page 45). Press toward the borders.

3. Quilt, bind, and enjoy! (See Quiltmaking Basics, pages 45–47.)

Quilt Assembly Diagram

ALTERNATE QUILT SIZES	TWIN	FULL/ QUEEN	KING
Number of blocks	40	80	110
Number of blocks wide by long	5 × 8	8 × 10	10 × 11
Finished size	60" × 87"	87" × 105"	105" × 114"
YARDAGE			
Light fat quarters	8	16	22
Pink fat quarters	8	16	22
Red fat quarters	8	16	22
Brown fat quarters	8	16	22
Inner border	½ yard	⅝ yard	¾ yard
Outer border	1⅝ yards	2 yards	2¼ yards
Binding	⅔ yard	⅞ yard	1 yard
Backing	5⅜ yards	8 yards	10¼ yards
Batting	68" × 95"	95" × 113"	113" × 122"

Bridge

Designed and made by Monique Dillard.
Quilted by LeAnne Olson.

FINISHED BLOCK: 9″ × 9″
FINISHED QUILT (as shown): 36½″ × 36½″

Materials

- Light fabric: 3 fat quarters
- Blue fabric: 1 fat quarter
- Brown fabric: 1 fat quarter
- Inner border: ¼ yard
- Outer border and binding: 1⅛ yards
- Backing: 1⅓ yards
- Batting: 42″ × 42″
- Optional: Fit to be Geese ruler (page 5)

Cutting Instructions

LIGHT FAT QUARTERS
Fit to be Geese method

- From 1 light fat quarter:

  Cut 3 strips 3½″ × width of fabric; cut into 8 pieces 3½″ × 4½″ (F), 4 squares 3½″ × 3½″ (G), and 2 squares 2¾″ × 2¾″, cut each diagonally once (A).

  Cut 2 strips 2¾″ × width of fabric; cut into 14 squares 2¾″ × 2¾″, and cut each diagonally once (A).

OR

Traditional method

- From 1 light fat quarter:

  Cut 3 strips 3½″ × width of fabric; cut into 8 pieces 3½″ × 4½″ (F), 4 squares 3½″ × 3½″ (G), and 2 squares 2″ × 2″ (A).

  Cut 3 strips 2″ × width of fabric; cut into 30 squares 2″ × 2″ (A).

- From each of the 2 remaining light fat quarters:

  Cut 1 square 16″ × 16″, and cut diagonally once for setting triangles.

BLUE FAT QUARTER
Fit to be Geese method

- From the blue fat quarter:

  Cut 2 strips 4½″ × width of fabric; cut into 8 squares 4½″ × 4½″, and cut each diagonally twice (B).

  Cut 2 strips 2″ × width of fabric; cut into 16 squares 2″ × 2″ (E).

OR

Traditional method

- From the blue fat quarter:

  Cut 3 strips 3½″ × width of fabric; cut into 30 pieces 2″ × 3½″ (B).

  Cut 2 strips 2″ × width of fabric; cut into 2 pieces 2″ × 3½″ (B) and 16 squares 2″ × 2″ (E).

BROWN FAT QUARTER
Fit to be Geese method

- From the brown fat quarter:

  Cut 3 strips 2¾″ × width of fabric; cut into 16 squares 2¾″ × 2¾″, and cut each diagonally once (C).

  Cut 2 strips 3″ × width of fabric; cut into 16 pieces 2″ × 3″ (D).

OR

Traditional method

- From the brown fat quarter:

  Cut 4 strips 2″ × width of fabric; cut into 32 squares 2″ × 2″ (C).

  Cut 2 strips 3″ × width of fabric; cut into 16 pieces 3″ × 2″ (D).

INNER BORDER

- Cut 4 strips 1½″ × width of fabric.

OUTER BORDER AND BINDING

- Cut 4 strips 5″ × width of fabric.
- Cut 4 strips 2¼″ × width of fabric.

Piecing

1. Make 16 Flying Geese units measuring 2″ × 3½″ using the light and blue fabrics.

For the Fit to be Geese method (page 5), use 32 light triangles cut from 2¾″ × 2¾″ squares cut diagonally once (A) and 16 blue triangles cut from 4 squares 4½″ × 4½″ cut diagonally twice (B).

OR

For the traditional method (page 5), use 32 light 2″ × 2″ squares (A) and 16 blue 2″ × 3½″ pieces (B).

Make 16.

2. Make 16 Flying Geese units measuring 2″ × 3½″ using the brown and blue fabrics.

For the Fit to be Geese method (page 5), use 32 brown triangles cut from 2¾″ × 2¾″ squares cut diagonally once (C) and 16 blue triangles cut from 4 squares 4½" × 4½" cut diagonally twice (B).

OR

For the traditional method (page 5), use 32 brown 2" × 2" squares (C) and 16 blue 2" × 3½" pieces (B).

Make 16.

3. Sew the units from Steps 1 and 2 together. Press in the direction of the arrow. Square the resulting units to 3½" × 3½". Repeat to make a total of 16.

Make 16.

4. Sew a brown 2" × 3" piece (D) to a blue 2" × 2" square (E). Press toward the blue. Repeat to make a total of 16. Rotate one, and sew together as shown. Watch the placement of the squares. On the back of the piece, snip ¼" in the center seam so that you can press half the seam allowance up and the other half down. Make a total of 8.

Make 8.

Pressing directions

5. On the backs of the light 4½" × 3½" (F) pieces, use the 45° mark on your ruler to draw 2 diagonal lines as shown. Note that one line starts at the upper left corner, and the second line starts at the lower right corner. The lines must be at a 45° angle. Place the rectangles with the drawn lines right sides together on the pieces from Step 4. Sew exactly on the line, and cut ¼" in from the line. (Before cutting, check to make sure the sewn lines are in the correct direction.) Press toward the light fabric. Square to 3½" × 3½". Repeat to make a total of 16 squares. Note that there will be a small scrap of extra fabric between the cutting lines.

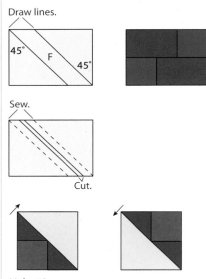

Draw lines.

Sew.

Cut.

Make 16.

6. Sew the block together using the pieces from Steps 3 and 5 and a 3½" × 3½" light square (G) for the middle of the block. Press in the direction of the arrows. Square the block to 9½" × 9½". Repeat to make a total of 4 blocks.

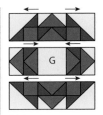

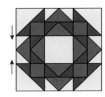

Make 4.

Quilt Construction

Refer to the quilt photo on page 36 and to the Quilt Assembly Diagram. Follow the arrows for pressing direction.

1. Arrange the blocks, and sew the quilt together in diagonal rows, using the blocks and the triangles cut from the 16" × 16" light squares. Press in the direction of the arrows. The setting triangles are larger than needed. Trim the edges of the quilt top to ¼" from the seams before sewing on the borders.

2. Sew on the inner border and then the outer border (see Borders, Quiltmaking Basics, page 45). Press toward the borders.

3. Quilt, bind, and enjoy! (See Quiltmaking Basics, pages 45–47)

Quilt Assembly Diagram

Cribbage

Designed and made by Monique Dillard.
Quilted by Sue Glorch.

FINISHED BLOCK: 4½″ × 4½″
FINISHED QUILT (as shown): 58″ × 76″, 140 blocks

Information for alternate quilt sizes is on page 41.

Materials

- Light fabric: 9 fat quarters
- Dark fabric: 9 fat quarters
- Inner border: ⅜ yard
- Outer border: 1½ yards
- Binding: ⅝ yard
- Backing: 4⅞ yards
- Batting: 66″ × 84″

Cutting Instructions

Before cutting, match the light and dark fat quarters into pairs, and cut the pairs with right sides together. Each light/dark pair makes 16 blocks.

LIGHT AND DARK FAT QUARTERS

- From each light/dark fat quarter pair:

  Cut 2 strips 5½″ × width of fabric; from each strip, cut 2 squares 5½″ × 5½″, 1 piece 3½″ × 9″, and 1 piece 2″ × 9″.

  Cut 3 strips 2″ × width of fabric; from 1 strip, cut 8 squares 2″ × 2″, and then cut the 2 remaining strips into 3 pieces 2″ × 10″.

INNER BORDER

- Cut 7 strips 1½″ × width of fabric.

OUTER BORDER

- Cut 7 strips 6″ × width of fabric.

BINDING

- Cut 8 strips 2½″ × width of fabric.

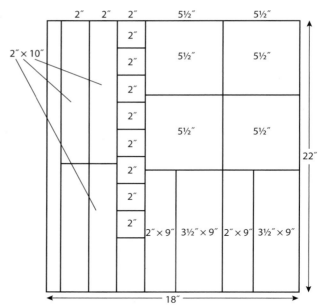

Fat Quarter Cutting Diagram

Piecing

1. Sew a 2″ × 10″ strip of light fabric to each side of a 2″ × 10″ strip of dark fabric. Press in the direction of the arrows. Cut the strip set into 4 segments 2″ wide from each pair of fat quarters.

Cut the pieces into 4 segments 2″ wide from each pair of fat quarters.

2. Sew a 2″ × 9″ strip of dark to a 3½″ × 9″ strip of light. Press in the direction of the arrow. Repeat to make 2 strip sets from each pair of fat quarters. Cut the strip sets into a total of 8 segments 2″ wide.

Make 2 sets and cut the pieces into 8 segments 2″ wide from each pair of fat quarters.

3. Sew a segment from Step 2 to each side of a segment from Step 1. Press in the direction of the arrows. Square the block to 5″ × 5″. Repeat to make a total of 4 from each light/dark fat quarter pair for the total number of blocks needed for your desired quilt size. (For the quilt as shown on page 39, make 36 blocks.).

Make 4 from each light/dark fat quarter pair.

4. Repeat Steps 1–3 reversing the lights and darks to make as may blocks a needed for your desired quilt size. (For the quilt as shown on page 39, make 36 blocks.)

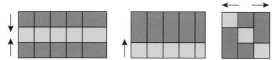

Make 4 from each light/dark fat quarter pair.

5. Make 8 Half-Square Triangles (page 5) from each light/dark fat quarter pair using 4 light 5½″ × 5½″ squares and 4 dark 5½″ × 5½″ squares. Trim the squares to 5″ × 5″.

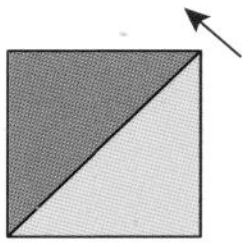

Make 8 from each light/dark fat quarter pair.

6. Draw a diagonal line from corner to corner on the back of each of the 2″ × 2″ light squares and the 2″ × 2″ dark squares. Place a 2″ × 2″ light square right sides together on the dark corner of a Half-Square Triangle from Step 5. Sew directly on the line. Press in the direction of the arrow, and trim the bottom 2 layers to ¼″. Place a 2″ × 2″ dark square right sides together on the light corner of the same Half-Square Triangle from Step 5. Sew directly on the line. Press in the direction of the arrow and trim the bottom 2 layers to ¼″. Repeat to make a total of 8 from each pair of light and dark fat quarters for the total number of blocks for your desired quilt size. (For the quilt as shown on page 39, make 72 blocks.)

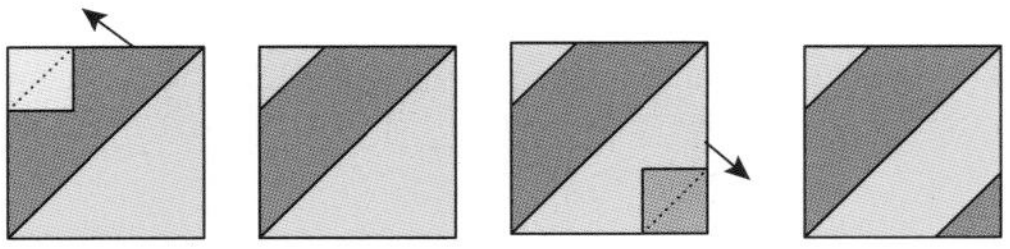

Make 8 from each light/dark fat quarter pair.

Quilt Construction

Refer to the quilt photo on page 39 and to the Quilt Assembly Diagram. Follow the arrows for pressing direction.

1. Arrange the blocks, and sew the quilt together in rows. Press in the direction of the arrows. Note that you will have extra blocks.

2. Sew on the inner border and then the outer border (see Borders, Quiltmaking Basics, page 45). Press toward the borders.

3. Quilt, bind, and enjoy! (See Quiltmaking Basics, page 45–47.)

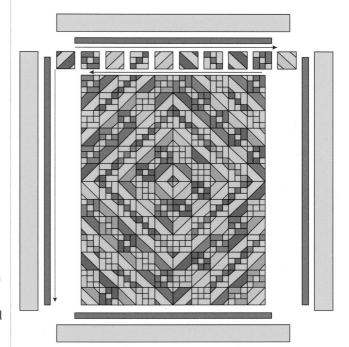

Quilt Assembly Diagram

ALTERNATE QUILT SIZES	TWIN	FULL/ QUEEN	KING
Number of blocks	160	320	484*
Number of blocks wide by long	10 × 16	16 × 20	22 × 22
Finished size	58″ × 85″	85″ × 103″	112″ × 112″
YARDAGE			
Light fat quarters	10	20	31
Dark fat quarters	10	20	31
Inner border	⅜ yard	½ yard	⅝ yard
Border	1½ yards	2 yards	2¼ yards
Binding	⅝ yard	¾ yard	1 yard
Backing	5⅓ yards	8 yards	10¼ yards
Batting	66″ × 93″	93″ × 111″	120″ × 120″

Note that you will have extra blocks for the king-size quilt.

Crazy Eights

Designed by Monique Dillard.
Made and quilted by Sue Glorch.

FINISHED BLOCK: 6″ × 6″
FINISHED QUILT (as shown): 60″ × 72″, 84 blocks
(4 of the blocks are used in the border)

Information for alternate quilt sizes is on page 44.

Materials

- Light fabric: 10 fat quarters
- Blue fabric: 10 fat quarters
- Red fabric: 10 fat quarters
- Border fabric: 1½ yards
- Binding: ⅝ yard
- Backing: 4 yards
- Batting: 68″ × 80″

Cutting Instructions

Before beginning, match the light, blue, and red fat quarters into sets for piecing. Cut the fat quarters separately. Each set will make 9 blocks.

LIGHT FAT QUARTERS

- From each light fat quarter:

  Cut 3 strips 3½″ × width of fabric; cut into 30 pieces 3½″ × 2″ (A).

  Cut 3 strips 2″ × width of fabric; cut into 18 squares 2″ × 2″ (C) and 6 pieces 2″ × 3½″ (A).

BLUE FAT QUARTERS

- From each blue fat quarter:

  Cut 4 strips 2″ × width of fabric; cut into 18 squares 2″ × 2″ (D), and reserve the 2 leftover strips for Four-Patches.

RED FAT QUARTERS

- From each red fat quarter:

  Cut 6 strips 2″ × width of fabric; cut into 36 squares 2″ × 2″ (B), and reserve the 2 leftover strips for Four-Patches.

BORDER

- Cut 7 strips 6½″ × width of fabric.

BINDING

- Cut 7 strips 2¼″ × width of fabric.

Piecing

1. Sew a 2″ strip of blue fabric to a 2″ strip of red fabric. Press toward the blue. Repeat to make 2 strip sets. Cut both of the strip sets into 9 segments 2″ wide for a total of 18 segments from each pair of red and blue fat quarters.

Make 2 sets and cut into 18 segments 2″ wide from each pair of red and blue fat quarters.

2. Rotate 1 of the segments, and sew it to another to make a Four-Patch. Press in the direction of the arrow. Repeat to make 9 Four-Patches from each pair of red and blue fat quarters.

Make 9 from each pair of red and blue fat quarters.

3. On the back of each of the 2″ × 2″ red squares (B), draw a diagonal line from corner to corner. Select half of the 2″ × 2″ squares (B), and place them right sides together on 2″ × 3½″ light rectangles (A). Sew directly on the line, and press toward the red. Trim the bottom 2 layers to ¼″. Watch the placement of the red square and make sure the piece looks exactly as shown. Make 18 from each pair of red and light fat quarters.

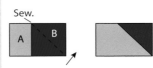

Use half of red 2″ × 2″ squares to make 18 from each red/light pair.

4. Use the remaining 2″ × 2″ red squares with drawn lines (B), and place them right sides together on the 2″ × 3½″ rectangles (A) of the same light fabric used in Step 3. Make sure that the diagonal line is heading in the opposite direction as in the pieces from Step 3. Sew directly on the line, and press toward the red. Trim the bottom layers to ¼″. Make 18 from each pair of red and light fat quarters.

Use remaining red 2″ × 2″ squares to make 18 from each red/light pair.

5. Sew the block together using a Four-Patch from Step 2, 2 pieces each from Steps 3 and 4, 2 light squares 2″ × 2″ (C), and 2 blue squares 2″ × 2″ (D). Press the block in the direction of the arrows. Square the block to 6½″ × 6½″. Repeat to make 9 blocks per color combination for the total number of blocks needed for your desired quilt size. (For the quilt as shown on page 42, make 90 blocks. Note that you will have 6 extra blocks.)

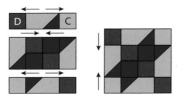

Make 9 per color combination.

Quilt Construction

Refer to the quilt photo on page 42 and to the Quilt Assembly Diagram. Follow the arrows for pressing direction.

1. Arrange the blocks, and sew the quilt together in rows. You will have leftover blocks. Press in the direction of the arrows.

2. Piece the strips together, and cut 2 border pieces 6½″ × 48½″ for the top borders and 2 border pieces 6½″ × 60½″ for the side borders. Sew the side borders to the quilt top, and press toward the border. Sew 4 of the leftover blocks to the ends of the top and bottom border pieces. Press toward the border. Sew these to the quilt top. Press toward the border.

3. Quilt, bind, and enjoy! (See Quiltmaking Basics, pages 45–47.)

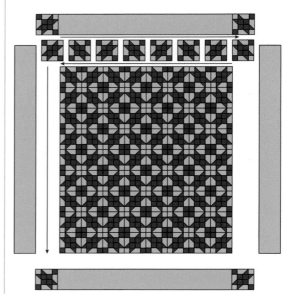

Quilt Assembly Diagram

ALTERNATE QUILT SIZES	TABLE RUNNER	TWIN	FULL/QUEEN	KING
Number of blocks	16 + 4 corners = 20*	117 + 4 corners = 121*	195 + 4 corners = 199*	289 + 4 corners = 293*
Number of blocks wide by long	2 × 8	9 × 13	13 × 15	17 × 17
Finished size	24″ × 60″	66″ × 90″	90″ × 102″	114″ × 114″
YARDAGE				
Light fat quarters	4**	14	23	33
Blue fat quarters	4**	14	23	33
Red fat quarters	4**	14	23	33
Border	1 yard	1⅝ yards	2 yards	2½ yards
Binding	½ yard	¾ yard	⅞ yard	1 yard
Backing	1⅞ yards	5½ yards	8⅓ yards	10⅓ yards
Batting	28″ × 64″	74″ × 98″	98″ × 110″	122″ × 122″

Note that you will have extra blocks for all sizes.

**Note that you need only 3 light fat quarters, 3 blue fat quarters, and 3 red fat quarters for the table runner, but having 4 of each will give you a better variety.*

  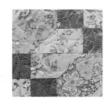   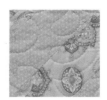

Quiltmaking Basics: How to Finish Your Quilt

General Guidelines

Seam Allowances

A ¼″ seam allowance is used for most projects. It's a good idea to do a test seam before you begin sewing to check that your ¼″ is accurate. Accuracy is the key to successful piecing.

Pressing

In general, press seams toward the darker fabric. Press lightly in an up-and-down motion. Avoid using a very hot iron or over-ironing, which can distort shapes and blocks. Be especially careful when pressing bias edges, as they stretch easily. Arrows are provided for pressing.

Borders

When border strips are cut on the crosswise grain, piece the strips together to achieve the needed lengths.

Butted Borders

In most cases the side borders are sewn on first. When you have finished the quilt top, measure it through the center vertically. This will be the length to cut the side borders. Place pins at the centers of all four sides of the quilt top, as well as in the center of each side border strip. Pin the side borders to the quilt top first, matching the center pins. Using a ¼″ seam allowance, sew the borders to the quilt top, and press toward the border.

Measure horizontally across the center of the quilt top, including the side borders. This will be the length to cut the top and bottom borders. Repeat the pinning, sewing, and pressing process outlined above.

Backing

Plan on making the backing a minimum of 8″ longer and wider than the quilt top. Piece, if necessary. Trim the selvages before you piece to the desired size.

Batting

The type of batting to use is a personal decision; consult your local quilt shop. Cut batting approximately 8″ longer and wider than your quilt top. Note that your batting choice will affect how much quilting is necessary. Check the manufacturer's instructions to see how far apart the quilting lines can be.

Basting

Basting keeps the quilt "sandwich" layers from shifting while you are quilting.

If you plan to machine quilt, pin baste the quilt layers together with safety pins placed a minimum of 3″–4″ apart. Begin basting in the center and move toward the edges, first in vertical, then horizontal, rows. Try not to pin directly on the intended quilting lines.

If you plan to hand quilt, baste the layers together with thread, using a long needle and light-colored thread. Knot one end of the thread. Using stitches approximately the length of the needle, begin in the center and move out toward the edges in vertical and horizontal rows approximately 4″ apart. Add two diagonal rows of basting.

Binding

Trim excess batting and backing from the quilt, even with the edges of the quilt top.

Double-Fold Straight-Grain Binding

Piece the binding strips together with diagonal seams to make a continuous binding strip. Trim the seam allowance to ¼". Press the seams open.

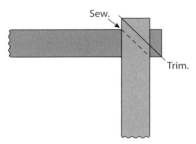

Sew from corner to corner.

Completed diagonal seam

Press the entire strip in half lengthwise, with wrong sides together. With raw edges even, start sewing the binding to the front edge of the quilt in the middle of one side of the quilt. Leave the first few inches of the binding unattached.

Stop ¼" away from the first corner (see Step 1), and back-stitch one stitch. Lift the presser foot and needle. Rotate the quilt a quarter-turn. Fold the binding at a right angle so it extends straight above the quilt and the fold forms a 45° angle in the corner (see Step 2). Then bring the binding

strip down even with the edge of the quilt (see Step 3). Begin sewing at the folded edge. Repeat in the same manner at all corners.

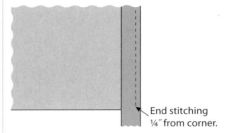

Step 1. Stitch to ¼" from corner.

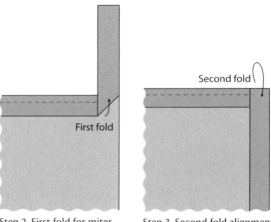

Step 2. First fold for miter   Step 3. Second fold alignment

Continue stitching until you are back near the beginning of the binding strip. See Finishing the Binding Ends for tips on finishing and hiding the raw edges of the ends of the binding.

Finishing the Binding Ends

Method 1:

After stitching around the quilt, fold under the beginning tail of the binding strip ¼" so that the raw edge will be inside the binding after it is turned to the back of the quilt. Place the end tail of the binding strip over the beginning folded end. Continue to attach the binding, and stitch slightly beyond the starting stitches. Trim the excess binding. Fold the binding over the raw edges to the quilt back, and hand stitch, mitering the corners.

Method 2:

Fold the ending tail of the binding back on itself where it meets the beginning binding tail. From the fold, measure and mark the cut width of the binding strip. Cut the ending binding tail to this measurement. For example, if the binding is cut 2¼" wide, measure 2¼" from the fold on the ending tail of the binding, and cut the binding tail to this length.

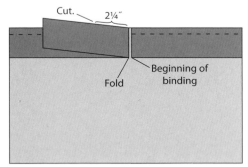

Cut binding tail.

Open both tails. Place one tail on top of the other tail at a right angle, with right sides together. Mark a diagonal line from corner to corner, and stitch on the line. Check that you've done it correctly and that the binding fits the quilt, and then trim the seam allowance to ¼". Press open.

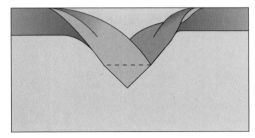

Stitch ends of binding diagonally.

Refold the binding and stitch this binding section in place on the quilt. Fold the binding over the raw edges to the quilt back, and hand stitch.

Note: For a short video on this technique, go to www. ctpub.com. Scroll down to the bottom of the page to *Consumer Resources* and click on *Quiltmaking Basics: Tips & Techniques for Quiltmaking and More*. Select *Completing a Binding with an Invisible Seam*.

About the Author

Monique Dillard of Rockford, Illinois, was born in Winnipeg, Manitoba, Canada. Her love of quilting was nurtured by relatives in Canada who taught her the art of handwork and sewing. She parlayed her degree in mathematics into a genuine understanding of the need for accurate ¼" seams, squared blocks, and precise cutting. She was a regular teacher at her local quilt shop for fifteen years until her budding quilt design business, Open Gate, steered her toward a national audience. These days, you can find Monique teaching across the United States at quilt guilds, quilt shows, and weekend retreats. Monique's classes always fill up quickly with fans from previous classes and students eager to learn from this talented designer.

Follow Monique at www.opengatequilts.com as she continues to create unique and creative quilt patterns, books, and rulers.

Resources

The Fit to be Geese ruler and Fit to be Square ruler are available for wholesale and retail sales through www.opengatequilts.com or directly from Monique Dillard at 1607 Charlotte Drive, Rockford, IL 61108.

the Quiltmaker's Club

More Patterns for Less

In this new series, we are gathering fabulous projects from established patternmakers into affordable books, all with the same high quality and accuracy you've come to expect from us. Now you get more patterns and more value!

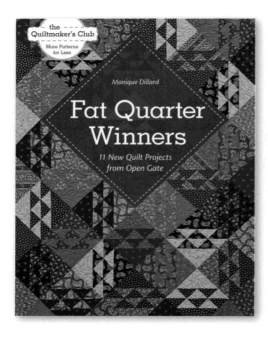

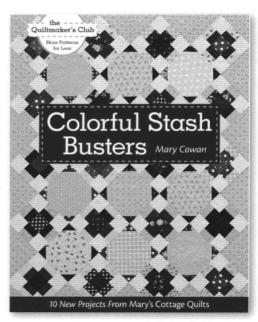

Available at your local retailer or **www.ctpub.com** *or* **800-284-1114 (USA)** ▪ **925-677-0377 (International)**

For a list of other fine books from C&T Publishing, visit our website to view our catalog online.

C&T PUBLISHING, INC.
P.O. Box 1456
Lafayette, CA 94549
800-284-1114

Email: ctinfo@ctpub.com
Website: www.ctpub.com

C&T Publishing's professional photography services are now available to the public. Visit us at www.ctmediaservices.com.

Tips and Techniques can be found at www.ctpub.com > Consumer Resources > Quiltmaking Basics: Tips & Techniques for Quiltmaking & More

For quilting supplies:

COTTON PATCH
1025 Brown Ave.
Lafayette, CA 94549
Store: 925-284-1177
Mail order: 925-283-7883

Email: CottonPa@aol.com
Website: www.quiltusa.com

Note: Fabrics used in the quilts shown may not be currently available, as fabric manufacturers keep most fabrics in print for only a short time.